Harriet Tubman

by Jill C. Wheeler

Breaking Barriers

visit us at
www.abdopub.com

Published by ABDO & Daughters, an imprint of ABDO
Publishing Company, 4940 Viking Drive, Suite 622, Edina,
Minnesota 55435. Copyright ©2003 by Abdo Consulting
Group, Inc. International copyrights reserved in all countries.
No part of this book may be reproduced in any form without
written permission from the publisher.

Printed in the United States.

Edited by Paul Joseph
Graphic Design: John Hamilton
Cover Design: Mighty Media
Interior Photos: AP/Photo, p. 7, 17, 26, 34, 37, 38, 40, 42, 48,
59, 61
Corbis, p. 1, 5, 6, 9, 10, 13, 14, 18, 21, 22, 25, 29, 30, 33, 39, 43,
45, 46, 55, 56, 60
Digital Stock, p. 51, 52

Library of Congress Cataloging-in-Publication Data

Wheeler, Jill C., 1964-
    Harriet Tubman / Jill C. Wheeler.
        p. cm. — (Breaking barriers)
        Summary: A biography of the African American woman
who spent her childhood in slavery and later worked to help other
slaves escape north to freedom through the Underground Railroad.
    Includes bibliographical references and index.
    ISBN 1-57765-908-2
    1. Tubman, Harriet, 1820?-1913—Juvenile literature. 2. Slaves—
United States—Biography—Juvenile literature. 3. African American
women—Biography—Juvenile literature. 4. Underground railroad—
Juvenile literature. 5. Antislavery movements—United States—
History—19th century—Juvenile literature. [1. Tubman, Harriet,
1820?-1913. 2. Slaves. 3. African Americans—Biography. 4.
Women—Biography. 5. Underground railroad.] I. Title.

E444.T82 W47 2003
973.7'115—dc21
[B]

                                                2002026097

Contents

A Trip through History

Many of the seventh and eighth graders at Albany Free School had read about the Underground Railroad. They knew it wasn't really a railroad at all. It was a network of people and places that helped slaves reach freedom from the late 1700s until the American Civil War.

In spring 2002, the students saw a new side of the Underground Railroad. They took a 13-day field trip through Maryland, Delaware, and Pennsylvania. They followed the escape route of a famous Underground Railroad conductor. A conductor was a person who led escaped slaves to freedom. This conductor had escaped from slavery herself before she began leading others to freedom.

The students visited cramped hiding places behind false walls. They heard stories of the hardships escaped slaves had faced. As they drove along the route, they thought about the slaves who had walked it so long ago.

Harriet Tubman

An undated woodcut of Harriet Tubman.

"I wouldn't have made it," said one seventh grader. Many slaves wouldn't have made it either, were it not for that famous conductor. Her name was Harriet Tubman. Nearly 100 years after her death, Tubman's story continues to amaze and inspire.

Tubman never went to school and never learned to read or write. Yet she outsmarted hundreds of slave owners and slave catchers. Tubman lived at a time when African-Americans and women were considered inferior. Yet she rose above these challenges to earn a place in American history.

A woman in Raisin Township, Michigan, shows off a hiding place underneath the wooden floorboards in her home. The house was built in the 1840s and was a stop on the Underground Railroad.

The Property Of...

Harriet Tubman was born into slavery as Araminta Ross in 1820 or 1821. She took the name Harriet as a teenager. Young Harriet was born in a windowless, one-room shack in Dorchester County, Maryland. She never knew her exact birth date because few slave owners recorded slave births.

Harriet was born to Benjamin Ross and Harriet "Rit" Greene. Benjamin, Rit, and their 11 children were the property of Edward Brodas. Brodas could do anything he wanted with his slaves, including selling them. "Every time I saw a white man I was afraid of being carried away," Harriet recalled. "I had two sisters carried away in a chain-gang—one of them left two children. We were always uneasy."

As property, slaves had no rights. They could be beaten or killed for no reason. While some slave owners treated their slaves well, others treated them like animals. Many slave owners believed that slaves were inferior. They believed they had a God-given right to treat their slaves any way they pleased.

Two slave children brought from Africa and sold in the United States.

A slave is shown being beaten and separated from his family.

As a small child, Harriet had few opportunities to run and play. "I grew up like a neglected weed," she said, "ignorant of liberty, having no experience of it." When Harriet was around five years old, she began her duties as a slave.

Slave owners sometimes hired out their slaves to make extra money. Several local people looking to hire slaves approached Brodas. Over the next few years, Harriet was hired out many times. Because she was so young, Brodas could offer her for very little money.

One time, he hired Harriet out to be a weaver's apprentice. She had to stay inside all day helping clean and wind yarn. The fuzz from the yarn and the dust in the workroom made her sneeze. Before, she'd been able to enjoy fresh air outside. Now she was forced to stay indoors. She no longer had her mother and father with her in the evenings. Now she had to sleep alone, curled up on the floor and shivering.

Harriet's new masters quickly realized she wasn't interested in learning to weave. They ordered her to check their muskrat traps instead. Harriet had to wade into waist-deep water every day to check the traps. One day, she had to go into the cold water just as she was coming down with the measles. She became very ill. Her new masters sent her home to her mother, who nursed Harriet back to health.

A Harsh Reality

When Harriet recovered, Brodas hired her out again. This time to a young woman called Miss Susan. Harriet's job was to take care of Miss Susan's baby and do household chores. Harriet had never done some of those chores before.

The first time Harriet was asked to sweep and dust a room, she did it wrong. After sweeping, she dusted right away. The dust from the sweeping settled on the furniture after she'd dusted. The room still looked undusted. Miss Susan screamed at her and told her to do it again.

Again and again, Harriet did it wrong. So Miss Susan reached for a whip and beat Harriet. Finally, Miss Susan's sister stepped in. She explained to Miss Susan that Harriet had not been told the right way to do things. Miss Susan's sister told Harriet to wait until the dust settled after sweeping, then dust the furniture. Harriet followed these instructions. The job then went perfectly.

Actress Cicely Tyson portrayed Harriet Tubman in the 1978 television movie, A Woman Called Moses.

This photo of African-American slave children from North Carolina was taken in 1862 or 1863, during the Civil War.

After a long day of chores, Harriet had to watch the baby. "I was so little I had to sit on the floor and have the baby put in my lap," Harriet remembered. "That baby was always in my lap except when it was asleep or its mother was feeding it." At night, Harriet had to rock the baby's cradle so it wouldn't cry. Sometimes she fell asleep and the baby cried. The baby's cries woke Miss Susan, and she lashed Harriet with a whip. Harriet carried the scars from that whip all her life.

Miss Susan eventually returned Harriet to Brodas. By then, Harriet was thin from hunger and suffering from overwork and lack of sleep. Rit was delighted to have her daughter back home. Once again, she nursed Harriet back to health.

Rit hoped Harriet would be trained as a house slave. Slaves who worked in their master's homes usually had better working conditions and better treatment. Slaves who worked in the fields had to labor long hours in miserable conditions. Yet Harriet seemed too rebellious to be a house slave. So Harriet's master hired her out to a man who needed someone to chop and load wood. Though still a child, Harriet began to do the work of an adult.

Harriet continued working outside and in the fields. As she neared her teens, she replaced the long shirt she wore with a long dress and wrapped a bandanna around her head.

Seeds of Rebellion

When Harriet was an adult, she worked in the fields beside the other adult slaves. They taught her how to do field work. They also taught her religious songs, called spirituals. She listened to their legends and superstitions. And they whispered about a railroad no one could see. It was a railroad that could whisk a slave north to freedom.

Harriet was interested in the tales of slaves that ran away to freedom. She hated slavery and wanted freedom for herself. One day when she was about 14, she saw a slave named Jim slip away from the group. She followed him, thinking he might be heading for the mysterious railroad.

The overseer saw Jim about the same time that Harriet did. He, too, went after Jim. They followed Jim to a local store. The overseer asked Harriet to help tie Jim up so he could whip him. Harriet refused. She stood between Jim and the overseer as Jim edged toward the door of the store.

New slaves are led through a city street on their way to market prior to the Civil War.

Young men in chains re-enact the slave trade during a living history demonstration.

The overseer became so angry he grabbed a heavy weight from the store counter. He threw it toward Jim. But the weight hit Harriet in the forehead. She crumpled to the floor.

The two-pound (1-kg) weight had pushed part of Harriet's skull into her brain. For months she lay on the floor of her family's cabin. Most of the time she slept. Other times she cried out in pain. Most people thought she would die.

Harriet's master looked in on her every now and then. He wanted to sell her. But he was afraid no one would buy an injured slave. "All the time he was bringing men to look at me and they stood there saying what they would give and what they would take," Harriet remembers. "They wouldn't give a sixpence for me."

Harriet eventually recovered enough to go back to work. For the rest of her life, she had a dent in her forehead from the overseer's rage. The brain injury caused Harriet to have frequent narcoleptic seizures. She would suddenly fall asleep, no matter what she was doing. Sometimes she fell asleep while speaking. When Harriet woke, she would continue whatever she had been doing as if there had been no interruption.

Hired Out

Harriet prayed a lot during her recovery. Her family was very religious, and Harriet was, too. At first she prayed that her master would have a change of heart and free his slaves. But Brodas died without freeing them. Now Harriet had another fear. There was a chance she or her other family members would be hauled away and sold.

Fortunately, Harriet and her family were not sold. Harriet went to work for a new master, who allowed her to hire her time. Slaves who hired their time could keep a portion of the money they made. Harriet hired herself out driving oxen, plowing, and doing other heavy work. One year, she made enough money to buy her own team of oxen. Another time, she worked for her father, cutting and stacking firewood.

In 1844, Harriet received permission to marry John Tubman. John was a freed slave, so he could come and go as he pleased. He had the right to get a job. Wherever he went, he had to carry the papers that decreed he was free. Freed slaves were always in danger of being captured and forced back into slavery.

African-American actors portray slaves in a historical re-enactment at Carter's Grove in Williamsburg, Virginia.

In Madison Co. Court!
LARGE SALE OF
LAND AND NEGROES

Petition for Sale of Land and Slaves.

Albert G. McClellan and others

vs.

Mary Vaden and husband, G. W. Vaden and others, distributees of Isabella McClellan, dec'd.

In the above cause, the undersigned, Clerk of the County Court of Madison county, Tenn., as commissioner, will expose to public sale on Saturday, 24th of March next, at the Court house, in the town of Jackson, that most desirable and conveniently situated Tract of Land, known as the McClellan farm, containing

1000 ACRES.

in one body, and lying within a mile and a half of the town of Jackson. Also, at the same time and place,

18 Or 20 NEGROES,

consisting of men, women and children. The land will be divided into tracts previous to the day of sale, and each division will be sold seperately.

Terms of sale.—Land on a credit of one and two years, and the negroes upon a credit of 12 months from the day of sale. Notes, with good security, will be required of purchasers, and lien retained on both land and negroes for the purchase money. Title t. the land and negroes indisputable.

P. C. McCOWAT,
C. & M. Commissioner

Feb. 24, 1860.

A notice giving details of a land and slave auction in 1860.

Harriet envied her husband's freedom. It made her even more determined to win her own. She began to talk to John about running north, where slavery was illegal. But John didn't want to go. Harriet also mentioned it to her father, Benjamin.

Benjamin didn't want Harriet to run. He knew many slaves were captured and killed when they tried to escape. But he also knew his daughter and her strong will. So he never talked with her about running, but he began to teach her things he thought she should know. He taught her how moss grows thicker on the north side of trees. He taught her which berries were good to eat and which plants could be used as medicine. He also taught her how to use the North Star as a compass.

Harriet hired herself out for the next five years. Then Harriet's owner died in 1849. As she had feared, she heard that all of the farm's slaves were to be sold. It was likely the slaves would be sent farther south. Harriet knew that, if she were going to escape, she would have to leave soon.

"I had reasoned this out in my mind," she remembered. "There was one of two things I had a *right* to, liberty, or death, if I could not have one, I would have the other."

On the Run

Harriet Tubman knew her family would be questioned when she disappeared. So she couldn't tell them her plans. But before she left, she was heard singing a spiritual. The song included the lines, "I'm bound for the promised land, friends, I'm going to leave you." It was a code to tell the other slaves that she was getting ready to flee. Throughout her life, she and other slaves used codes to communicate. They exchanged messages even within earshot of their owners and overseers.

No one knows exactly what route Tubman used to escape. She kept many secrets to remain safe from slave owners and slave catchers. Historians believe a local Quaker woman aided Tubman's escape. Members of the Quaker religion opposed slavery. Many Quakers helped slaves escape via the Underground Railroad. It is believed Tubman gave a handmade quilt to the Quaker woman, who in turn told her how to connect to the railroad.

This monument to the ending of slavery is on the Caribbean island of Barbados.

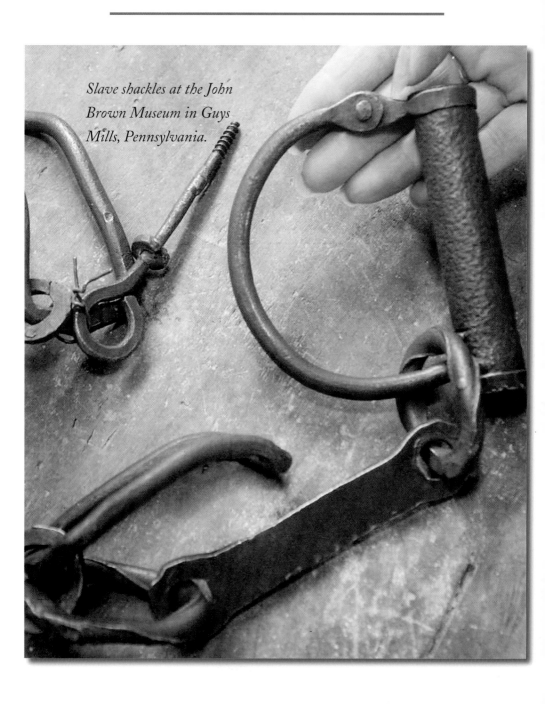

Slave shackles at the John Brown Museum in Guys Mills, Pennsylvania.

Tubman used the Underground Railroad to move north. The Underground Railroad wasn't a real railroad at all. People called it that because it seemed like slaves could escape as easily as if they'd boarded a train. Instead, the Underground Railroad was a series of homes and churches where slaves could get food, protection, and directions to the next house, or station. Many of the people involved with the railroad were African-American.

Tubman also had to rely on her wits. She followed the North Star as she headed north. And she traveled mainly at night to avoid anyone who was looking for her. She frequently waded through streams and swamps, so the water would cover her tracks.

After traveling nearly two weeks, she crossed the border into Pennsylvania. She was free. "When I found I had crossed that *line*, I looked at my hands to see if I was the same person," Tubman said later. "There was such a glory over everything; the sun came like gold through the trees, and over the fields, and I felt like I was in Heaven."

A New Mission

Freedom may have been heaven, but it was also strange. Suddenly, Tubman was in a new place where she didn't know anyone. All she knew was that she had to share the freedom she had found. "I was a stranger in a strange land; and my home, after all, was down in Maryland; because my father, my mother, my brothers, and sisters, and friends were there," she recalled. "I was free, and *they* should be free also; I would make a home in the North and bring them there."

Harriet got a job working in a hotel. For the first time, she could keep all the money she earned. Plus, if she didn't like the job, she could go work somewhere else. Sometimes she worked as a cook, sometimes as a maid. She saved her money and made plans for a trip back to Maryland. She wanted to lead her family to freedom.

Her mission began just a year after her own escape. It is believed Tubman learned that one of her sisters, Mary Ann, was about to be sold. Tubman found someone to deliver a message to Mary Ann's husband, a free man named John Bowley. Tubman told Bowley to take Mary Ann and their two children to Baltimore. Tubman would meet them there and take them the rest of the way to freedom.

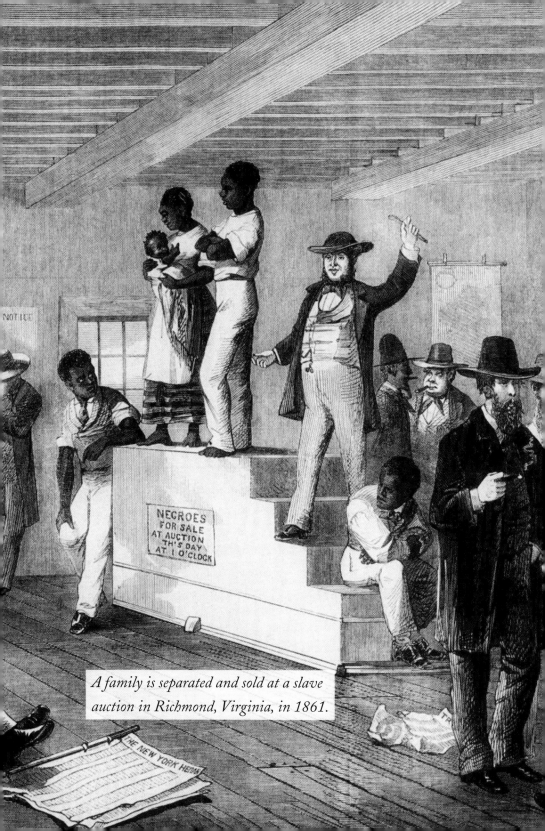

A family is separated and sold at a slave auction in Richmond, Virginia, in 1861.

Escaped slaves who were captured faced severe punishment by their owners.

Tubman's plans were almost destroyed. Mary Ann's master decided to sell her on the day she was to escape. Fortunately, Bowley found a way to abduct Mary Ann after she'd been auctioned off. Bowley helped his family get to Baltimore, where they met Tubman.

Baltimore was a dangerous place for an escaped slave. It was thick with slave catchers. Tubman herself had only escaped the year before. There may have been people still looking for her. Somehow Tubman managed to find a way for the group to travel without being spotted. She took them to Canada. It was the first of many rescues for Tubman.

The next year, Tubman returned to Maryland to free one of her brothers and two other men. Later that year, she went all the way back to her home in Dorchester County to get her husband. When she arrived, she learned that John Tubman had married another woman. Tubman tried not to get angry or feel sad. Instead, she found some more fugitives eager for freedom. She safely escorted them north to Philadelphia.

The Fugitive Slave Act

Tubman became free and relatively safe in 1849, when she crossed the state line into Pennsylvania. That changed in September 1850, when Congress passed a second Fugitive Slave Act.

The original Fugitive Slave Act was passed in 1793. It gave federal judges the right to determine if an escaped slave should be returned to his or her master. Accused slaves didn't receive a trial by jury if they were captured.

Many people in the North objected to the law. They said it violated the United States Constitution. The Constitution guarantees that people will receive a trial by a jury. In addition, many people in the North believed slavery was wrong. As a result, most northerners didn't enforce the first Fugitive Slave Act.

Meanwhile, southern slave owners felt their rights were being violated. Slaves were property and worth a lot of money. When a slave ran away, it was as if someone had stolen property. Southern slave owners pressured Congress to do something. So they passed the 1850 Fugitive Slave Act.

An actor plays the role of a slave at Carter's Grove slave quarters in Williamsburg, Virginia.

A poster printed in Boston, Massachusetts, warning African-Americans to beware of kidnappers and slave catchers.

The new law said escaped slaves must be returned to their owners. It stated that no one could help escaped slaves. Those that did would be punished. The new law also put slaves' fates into the hands of special county commissioners. The commissioners decided if an escaped slave should be returned or freed. The accused slaves couldn't speak in their own defense. Commissioners received $5 for every escaped slave they set free. They received $10 for every escaped slave they returned to the owner. Worse yet, any black person could be accused of being a fugitive slave. Even freed slaves were in danger of being returned to slavery.

It was clear the law was designed to help owners, not slaves. Tubman and other abolitionists were angry. Tubman now had no choice but to lead escaped slaves to Canada. Queen Victoria had proclaimed, in 1833, that all people of color living in Canada were free. "I wouldn't trust Uncle Sam with my people no longer," Harriet recalled. "But I brought them all clear off to Canada."

Tubman made a fourth trip south to rescue another of her brothers, his wife, and nine others. She led them all the way from Dorchester County, Maryland, to St. Catharines, Ontario, in Canada. Now she had to travel twice as far to lead the slaves to freedom. She realized she needed help to continue.

Workin' on the Railroad

Tubman soon met an African-American man named William Still. Still worked with the General Vigilance Committee of Philadelphia. The committee was an abolitionist group set up to help slaves after the Fugitive Slave Act was passed. The committee also provided one of the main stations on the Underground Railroad.

Still knew the workings of the Railroad very well. He knew which churches were stations and who had homes with false walls and hidden rooms. He knew who could provide fake transportation documents and false identification papers.

Still found Tubman was a natural conductor. Tubman had the intelligence, cunning, and planning abilities necessary to carry out dangerous missions. She also had the courage and strength to endure hardships and face risks. Tubman became one of the most successful conductors in the Underground Railroad.

A pastor at Emmanuel Episcopal Church in Cumberland, Maryland, walks through a secret tunnel below the church. Emmanuel Episcopal Church was the last stop for many on the Underground Railroad.

Tubman planned her missions like strategic military operations. She learned to lead people away on Saturday nights. Many slaves didn't have to work on Sundays. Even if the owners discovered they were missing on a Sunday, they were out of luck. Sunday was the one day of the week they couldn't print a missing notice. By the time the word got out, the slaves would have had an extra day to travel. Sometimes Tubman even hired people to follow the owner as he posted bills along the route north. The person following would tear the notices off the fence posts and buildings after the owner posted them.

A man looks out from behind a fake bookshelf at an Underground Railroad museum in Lakeshore Township, Ontario.

People help escaping slaves on Levi Coffin's Indiana farm, a major station of the Underground Railroad.

Tubman also learned how to outwit the slave catchers who chased after runaway slaves. She made sudden changes in direction to confuse her pursuers. She used disguises to move freely in slave territory. Often she dressed as an old woman and wandered country roads, singing. Slave owners saw a harmless old woman singing to herself. In reality, she was singing out coded instructions to the runaways who were hiding along the road.

Tubman became known as Moses in the slave community. Like Moses in the Bible, she led her people to freedom. Like Moses, she believed God was directing her. Tubman often spoke of her mission as being God's will for her life.

FIFTY DOLLARS
REWARD.

Ran away from Mount Welby, Prince George's County, Maryland, on Monday, the 2d inst., a negro man calling himself Joe Bond, about 25 years of age, about 5 feet 6 inchesin height, stout built, copper complexion; the only mark recollected is a peculiar speck in one of his eyes. Had on when he went away a frock tweed coat, dark brown, and cap near the same color. I will give twenty-five dollars if taken in Prince George's County, Md., or in Alexandria County, Virginia; and fifty dollars if taken elsewhere and returned to me, or secured so that I get him again.

T. R. EDELA

Piscataway, Prince George's, December 5. 1850.

This handbill from 1850 shows what runaway slaves faced as they made their way through Connecticut to Canada and freedom. By 1850, Connecticut had a well-established Underground Railroad that helped hundreds of slaves to freedom.

She also claimed that God guided her in her missions. Sometimes, it seemed that was true. Once she abruptly changed course for no particular reason. Later, she and her party learned that slave catchers had been waiting along the original route.

Tubman quickly adopted the name Moses. In later years, she would often go by Moses when speaking in public to protect her identity. Maryland slave owners hated this mysterious Moses. It was as if someone was systematically stealing their most valuable slaves.

Trained, adult slaves were worth between $1,000 and $2,000 each. All that money was slipping away, and the owners seemed powerless to do anything about it. Some offered rewards for Tubman's capture. The rewards are believed to have once totaled $40,000. That would be equal to about $1 million today.

Tubman once woke from one of her sleeping spells and heard two men discussing a poster that sought her capture. She quickly picked up a book and pretended to read. The men saw that she was reading and decided she couldn't be Tubman, because Tubman couldn't read. Meanwhile, Tubman prayed that she had the book right side up!

A side door leading to the basement of Graue Mill in Oak Brook, Illinois, is believed to have been used as an entrance for slaves at this Underground Railroad stop.

Sometimes Tubman's problems came from the slaves she was trying to help. Occasionally, slaves had second thoughts about fleeing. Tubman would tell them either they could continue north, or she would kill them. Any slave who had been with her would know her methods and routes. She couldn't risk that knowledge getting into the wrong hands.

Sometimes Tubman had to conduct women with babies. She always kept a sedative with her to give the babies so they wouldn't cry. Often, she carried the babies herself in a bag around her neck and shoulder. In 19 trips, she successfully freed more than 300 slaves. Moses, people whispered, never lost a soul.

Harriet Tubman, left, holding a pan, was photographed with a group of slaves she helped escape.

With the Abolitionists

Tubman moved her home from Philadelphia to St. Catharines after the Fugitive Slave Act was passed. She used her new home as a base from which newly escaped slaves could find work and get settled. Tubman felt that helping escaped slaves find work and housing was almost as important as freeing them.

In 1857, she helped her elderly parents escape to Canada. The rescue involved constructing a makeshift buggy from an old axle and some boards. It also meant traveling during the day. By now, Tubman knew her enemy so well she could outwit them easily. She was successful, and now her parents were free.

Tubman's success led to many friendships with important people. She became a popular speaker on the issue of slavery. Even though some of her masters had mistreated her, she refused to blame slave owners. "They don't know no better," she said. "They acts up to the light they have," meaning they do as they were brought up to do.

Sojourner Truth, whose legal name was Isabella Van Wagener, was born into slavery but later freed. She worked as an abolitionist and a suffragette, and was a leader of the Underground Railroad.

Frederick Douglass

Tubman's abolitionist friends included former New York Governor William Seward. Seward later became secretary of state for President Abraham Lincoln. Tubman got help from Quaker businessman Thomas Garrett. Garrett is credited with helping some 2,000 slaves to freedom.

Tubman also knew and received help from Frederick Douglass. Douglass was an escaped slave who founded an abolitionist newspaper. She also knew radical abolitionist John Brown. Brown's goal was to lead a rebellion of slaves to help overturn slavery.

Brown planned to raid the federal arsenal at Harpers Ferry, Virginia, to get guns for his rebellion. He knew he needed the support of the African-American community. He turned to Tubman for that. Tubman advised him on which routes to take and where he might get help. Brown called her General Tubman. He said she was "one of the best and bravest persons on this continent."

Abolitionist John Brown

The Harpers Ferry raid failed. The government hanged Brown for treason in December 1859. However, Tubman always respected him. She saw him as an important soldier in the war against slavery.

The Harpers Ferry raid further heightened the tensions between the North and the South. Tubman made her last rescue in December 1860. South Carolina seceded from the Union that same month. The American Civil War was about to begin.

The burning of the United States Arsenal at Harpers Ferry on April 18, 1861.

In the Army

Tubman and her parents had moved from St. Catharines to Auburn, New York, in 1859. With war just around the corner, her friends feared she might be in great danger. It was possible she could be captured and used by the North as a bargaining tool with the South. So she returned to Canada in 1860.

Tubman returned to the North in the spring of 1861. By this time, six more states had seceded from the Union. The Civil War began in April 1861, when Confederate forces attacked Fort Sumter in South Carolina. Tubman received permission to help the Union army in South Carolina.

Her first wartime duties were in a hospital for escaped slaves. Many slaves took advantage of the war to escape to the Union army. Tubman served as the army's liaison. As a former slave, she could understand what they had been through. She nursed the slaves back to health. She received $200 from the army and started a washhouse. There she taught women how to do laundry so they could earn their own money.

Taylor, an African-American drummer boy for the Union army.

Union soldiers wait at a rail station to be taken to the battlefield.

Aside from the first $200, Tubman received no other money from the army during the war. So at night she baked pies and made root beer. She sold the goods during the day to support herself and her work.

As the war progressed, Tubman became a spy and a scout for the Union Army. Few people suspected someone who looked like a tired old woman was a spy. They didn't realize it was Tubman, gathering valuable information about the enemy.

Tubman also recruited escaped slaves to be scouts. They would tell the army what they knew about the area they had just escaped from. Tubman even helped the army recruit African-Americans to fight. She used the skills she had learned through the Underground Railroad to sneak behind enemy lines and seek out trustworthy slaves. Escaping Confederate sentries was no more difficult for Tubman than escaping slave catchers.

In 1863, Tubman participated in the successful raid at South Carolina's Combahee River. She and her scouts helped Colonel James Montgomery plan the attack. They also rescued nearly 800 slaves that had been freed by the Emancipation Proclamation. Many of them joined the Union army.

Helping the Needy

Tubman spent three years helping the army during the Civil War. In 1864, she returned to Auburn. She was exhausted from years on the front lines, and her sleeping spells became worse. She needed a break. She also had to care for her aging parents. Fortunately, she had many friends in Auburn to help her.

The Civil War ended in 1865. Harriet returned south for a while to work at a government hospital in Virginia. She treated wounded soldiers with her knowledge of herbal remedies.

Later, Tubman's friends urged her to seek the money the army owed her. She had served much like a soldier, yet with no pay. Plus, her recruitment of soldiers alone was worth $1,800. The army consistently refused.

The view inside a ward of the Armory Square Hospital in Washington, D.C., during the American Civil War.

Harriet Tubman's home in Auburn, New York.

Tubman had no choice but to fund her activities with hard work and donations. Friends recalled that Tubman rarely had any money because she gave it away to anyone in need. She tried to help every poor, former slave who showed up on her doorstep. Her house in Auburn was usually full of people in need.

One day, a special person showed up at Tubman's house. His name was Nelson Davis, and he and Tubman had met during the war. Davis had served in the Union army. He was many years younger than Tubman, but he had always admired her. The two were married in 1869.

Tubman and Davis settled down in the small house she purchased. She grew a garden there and sold the vegetables to earn money. Her goal was to get enough money to open a home for aging African-Americans.

As the years went by, Tubman became involved in a new cause. She became interested in women's rights. In the late 1860s, a woman named Susan B. Anthony led a movement to give women the right to vote. It was the women's suffrage movement. Suffrage is another term for the right to vote. Anthony had been an abolitionist as well. Sadly, neither woman would live to see full voting rights for American women.

Final Days

Davis died from tuberculosis around 1888. In 1890, a pension act was passed that granted aid to veterans' widows. Tubman received $8 a month as Davis's widow. Because of her service in the army, several congressmen petitioned for an increase. When that increase was finally awarded, it was for $20 a month.

In 1896, Tubman bought 25 acres (10 ha) of land next to her home. But it was a struggle for her to make payments. So in 1903, Tubman gave her home and land to the local church she attended.

In 1908, the church opened the home for the needy that Tubman had wanted. However, the church wanted to turn away residents who had less than $100. Harriet didn't want to turn anyone away. The disagreement ended Tubman's involvement with the home. It closed shortly after her death.

Tubman developed pneumonia in March of 1913. Just days later, she died. The 93-year-old, illiterate, former slave was buried with full military honors in Auburn, New York. Finally, she had gone to her own Promised Land.

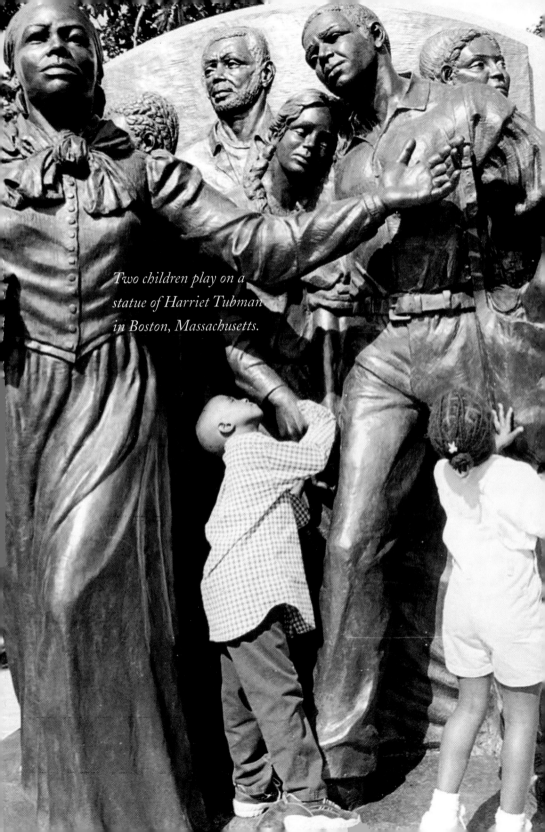

Two children play on a statue of Harriet Tubman in Boston, Massachusetts.

Timeline

1820 or 1821: Araminta Ross is born into slavery in Dorchester County, Maryland. As a teenager, she takes the name of Harriet, after her mother.

1844: Harriet marries John Tubman, a freed slave.

1849: Tubman leaves her husband and escapes to Pennsylvania. Later she joins the Underground Railroad movement, which helped slaves gain their freedom in the North.

1850: Tubman becomes a conductor on the Underground Railroad and helps groups of slaves escape to Canada. Later, she becomes known as "Moses."

1857: Tubman relocates with her parents to St. Catharines, Ontario.

1861: Tubman assists the Union Army during the Civil War. She helps sick and wounded former slaves recover and find jobs.

1869: Tubman marries Nelson Davis. They settle in Auburn, New York.

March 10, 1913: Harriet Tubman dies.

Web Sites

Would you like to learn more about Harriet Tubman? Please visit **www.abdopub.com** to find up-to-date Web site links about Harriet Tubman and the Underground Railroad. These links are routinely monitored and updated to provide the most current information available.

Slaves depicted in an Underground Railroad sculpture in Battle Creek, Michigan, are led to freedom by abolitionists Erastus Hussey and Harriet Tubman.

Glossary

abolitionist
A person who favors abolishing something. Before the Civil War, the abolitionists wanted to end slavery.

arsenal
A collection of weapons, or a place where weapons are made.

Confederate
A person loyal to the 11 slaveholding Southern states that seceded from the Union to form the Confederate States of America.

Emancipation Proclamation
A proclamation by President Abraham Lincoln that freed slaves in Confederate territory.

liaison
A person who helps with the communication between two groups or organizations.

narcolepsy
Brief attacks of deep sleep.

Quaker
A member of the religious group called the Society of Friends.

secede
To break away from a group.

seizure
A sudden attack caused by a disease or disorder.

sentries
Guards.

tuberculosis
A bacterial infection that primarily attacks the lungs.

Union
The states that remained in the United States during the Civil War.

Index